Edith Bloecher
Schwalm embroidery pattern book

1. edition 2017
ISBN-13: 978-1977831378
ISBN-10: 1977831370

Author, layout and photos:
Edith Bloecher
Groetzinger Str 71
D - 76227 Karlsruhe
www.handarbeitshaus.de
mailbox@handarbeitshaus.de
Tel: 0049 721 404717

CreateSpace, North Charleston, SC, USA
an Amazon.com Company
www.createspace.com

Print see last page

Schwalm Embroidery Pattern Book

Edith Bloecher

Content

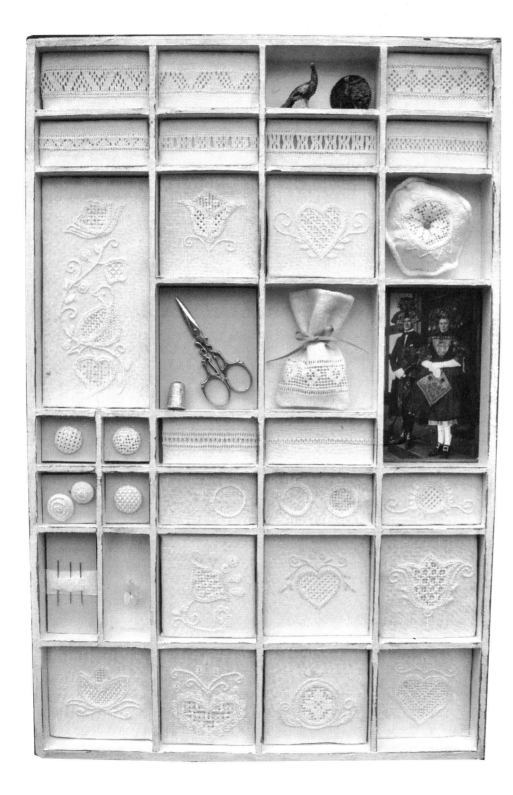

Letter case
with
Schwalm
embroidery

The numbers are the
pages with the
instructions

13	12		11
15	9	10	14
86	49	43	
		62	
103	17	7	
	48	41	55
44	54	27	42

3

Schwalm embroidery is the Hessian embroidery with certain defaults:

- The desired forms are: Heart, tulip, sun and bird, in addition tendrils and small sheets and perhaps a basket.
- These forms get first a border of coral stitches and of chain stitches . After that the inside is filled out with embroidery patterns.
- The tendrils are coral stitches and may not cross.
- And the whole has a certain style which corresponds to the tradition.

Because this book can have only a restricted number of pages, I keep to the tradition of the Schwalm embroidery. You may feel free for your work and also embroider other forms in your personal style. Then it is an embroidery in the style of the Hessian embroidery.

Here a picture of a historical Schwalm embroidery of a Schwalm national costume. The piece was white of course, but I bought it blue coloured.

The blouse sleeve had below inwards the embroidery and was surged up, so that this embroidery came around the upper arm. To the elbow the needleweaving hem, upwards the needlelace.

This old embroidery was embroidered on about 40ct linen.

THE MATERIAL TODAY

For the Schwälmer embroidery one uses normally a very fine close woven linen, but it goes on every countable fabric. It can also be an old farmer linen.

I use Weddigen linen 925, this is a fine 40ct linen or Newcastle of Zweigart, also 40ct, but a little more soft.

Also gladly used is Weddigen linen 160 with 34ct.

One embroiders with special embroidery thread / broder spécial in 16, 20, 25 and 30. One can also use crochet yarn 20, 30, 40.

I embroider with a pointed and a no pointed needle. I embroider the border with pointed needle, the threads drawing and the embroidering of the patterns with no pointed needle.

I prefer to embroider without embroidery frames, the linen is stable, but many use an embroidery ring or embroidery frame.

THE NEEDLEWEAVING HEM

Hemstitches are popular decorations, they subdivide the surface.

One weaves after the pattern around thread bundle of 3 or 4 threads. One can on the edge, the threads pre-bundle by hem-stitch, herringbone or four sided stitch, but this is not important.

With the historical Schwalm embroidery often one embroiders upperly and below the needleweaving hem a narrow hem-stitch. At the back one can keep there the thread ends.

Very small hem

4 threads are pulled out of the fabric first.

One encloses on top or below 1 x 6 threads and afterwards for the right small bar 3 x 3 threads.

A very useful narrow hemstitch which can be well embroidered around a doily

He is embroidered from left to right.

He does not need an edge fastening.

2. Needleweaving hem + 2 rows four sided stitch

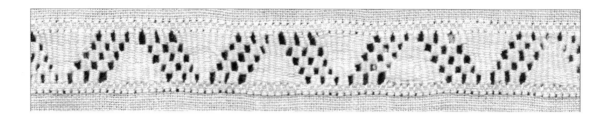

Draw threads:
1 thread out, 3 remain,
1 thread out, 2 remain,
20 threads out,
2 threads remain, 1 thread out,
3 remain,1 thread out.

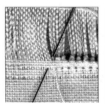 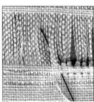 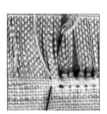

Four sided stitch:

With the four sided stitch one stitch behind diagonally, in front is the thread straight.1 four sided stitch exists of 3 oblique stitches.

Bundle and tighten tightly always 3 threads.

Vertical line = bundle of 3 threads

Horizontal line = once back and forth woven.

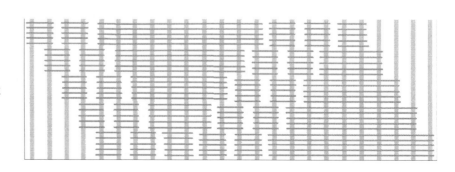

3. Needleweaving hem + 2 rows of four sided stitch variation

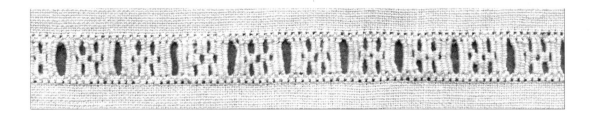

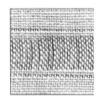

Draw threads:
1 thread out, 2 remain,
13 out,
2 remain, 1 thread out,

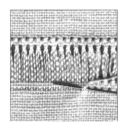 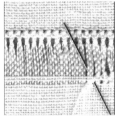 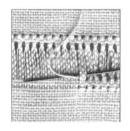

Four sided stitch variation

Very popular in vintage embroideries

One works from right to left.
Take 3 threads on the needle, stitch in the back diagonally
to the left above. Above take 3 threads on the needle .

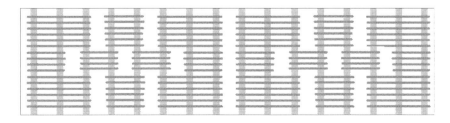

Vertical line = bundle of 3
threads

Horizontal line = once back and
forth woven.

4. Needleweaving hem + 2 rows of four sided stitch variation

Draw threads:
1 thread out, 2 remain,
13 threads out,
2 remain, 1 thread out.

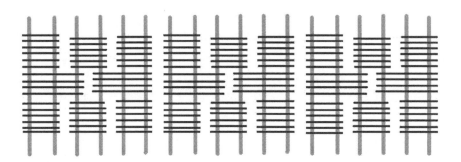

5. Needleweaving hem + shifted hem

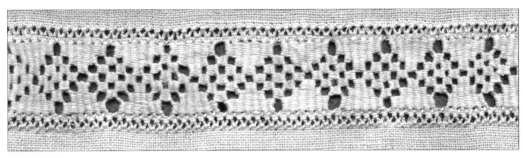

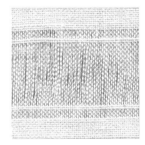

Draw threads:
4 threads out, 2 remain,
20 threads out,
2 remain, 4 threads out.

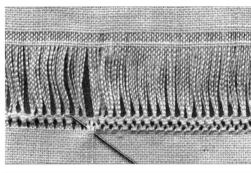

shifted hem

Embroider normal hemstitches on the outside over 4 fabric threads and at the narrow footbridge over 2 fabric threads. Work shifted.

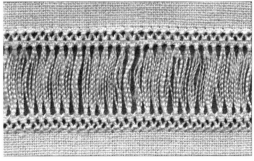

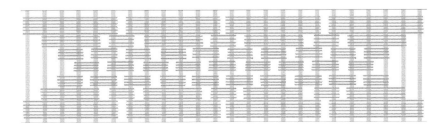

Vertical line = bundle of 3 threads

Horizontal line = once back and forth woven.

6. Needleweaving hem + 2 rows four sided stitch above and 2 below

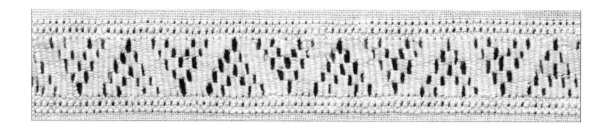

Draw threads:
1 thread out, 2 remain,
1 thread out, 2 remain,
20 threads out,
2 remain, 1 thread out,
2 remain, 1 thread out.

2 rows of four sided stitches or a variation of four sided stiches are embroidered on the edge here.

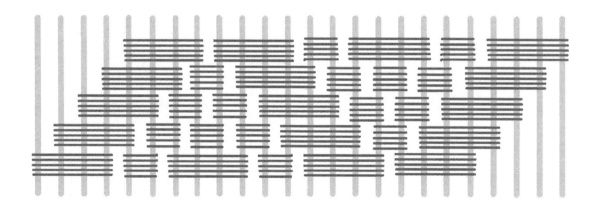

7. Needleweaving hem + 2 rows hem stitches

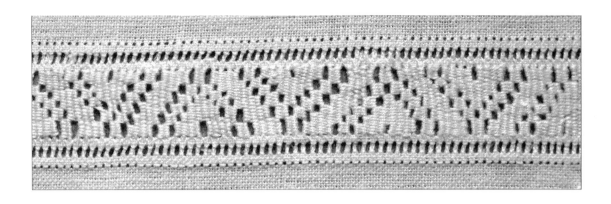

1 thread out,
3 remain,
4 threads out,
3 remain,
25 threads out,
3 remain,
4 threads out,
3 remain,
1 thread out.

Inside on 3 threads embroider the varied four sided stitch - see page 9
Outside make shadow stitches - see the description on this side here.

Begin below on the left, go down with the needle 3 threads more right and come out above on the left again, then go down 3 threads above on the right and come out below on the left again. In front you see back stitches, behind the threads cross to the herringbone stitch. Pull the threads.

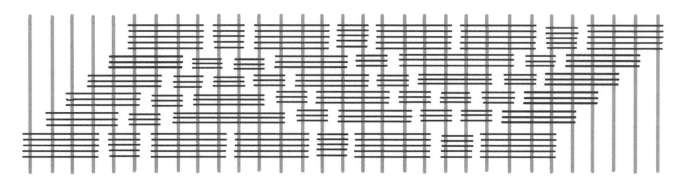

Pattern of needleweaving hem 7
One can weave 3 or 4 times back and forth.

8. Needleweaving hem + 2 rows of four sided stitch

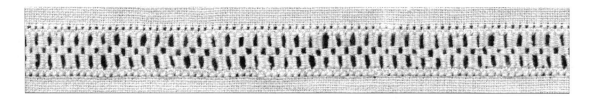

Draw threads:
1 thread out, 2 remain,
12 threads out,
2 remain, 1 thread out.

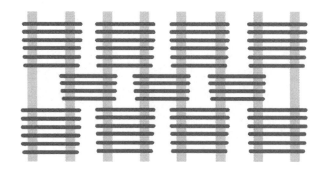

9. Needleweaving hem + 2 rows of four sided stitch variation

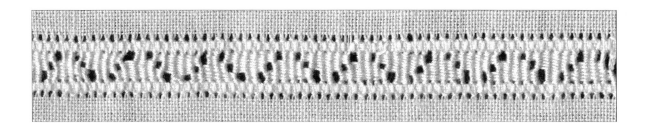

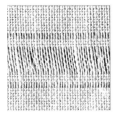

2 threads out,
3 remain,
10 threads out,
3 remain,
2 threads out.

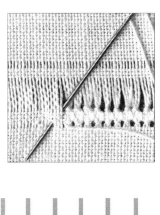
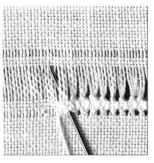
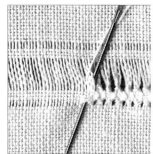

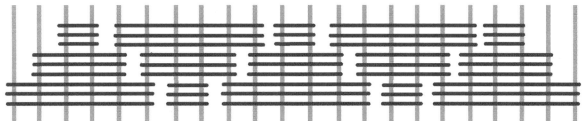

10. Historical needleweaving hem + satin stitch border

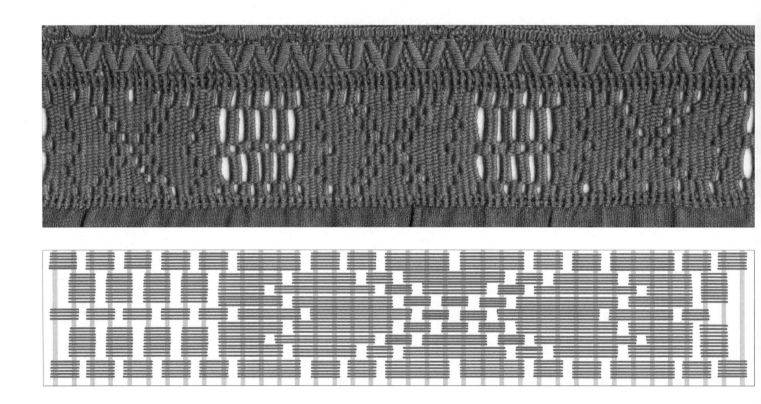

Approx. 30 threads are drawn for this needleweaving hem.

The border above the hemstitch is so far one sees
embroidered with satin stitches.

11. Peahole hem

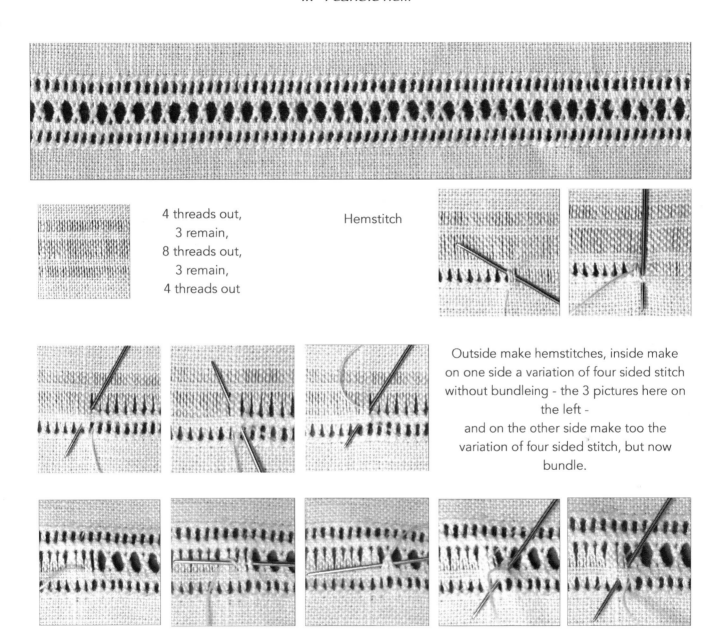

4 threads out,
3 remain,
8 threads out,
3 remain,
4 threads out

Hemstitch

Outside make hemstitches, inside make on one side a variation of four sided stitch without bundleing - the 3 pictures here on the left -
and on the other side make too the variation of four sided stitch, but now bundle.

The 3 pictures above: variation of four sided stitch, the 5 pictures below show how to bundle.

PLANNING AND DESIGN

I draw the patterns on the computer with the painting
program ArtRage 5. The version 5 has symmetrie.
Who like to know more, may ask me.

But if you like to design a pattern to yourselve, it is
also simply possible with templates.

The motives of the Schwalm embroidery are only
circle / sun, heart, tulip and bird.

For the circle search a round subject as a template, for
heart and tulip fold paper and cut the half motive and
a bird sign by hand.

Tendrils and leaves design free hand.

The forms are drawn with template.

One gets symmetrical tendrils by folding the paper and tracing of the tendril of the backside.

The more exact the better,, but manually exact to draw is heavy.

The needle:

One uses pointed and not pointed needles..

A pointed embroidery needle is suitable for the border with coral stitch and chain stitch.

For filling is a not pointed needle more pleasant.

Pattern transfer

Marking with pencil

A good possibility, because one can erase. But, for some time, new pencils have perhaps a resin which can be washed out no longer well. Therefore make either a wash test or take a pencil, which can be painted with water.

And it must not be a black pencil, a bright coloured pencil is less dominant.

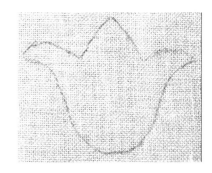

Marking with a water soluble pencil

If one makes the draft with templates or if one can see the draft through the linen, this is a simple and good possibility. For security sew the lines after marking with a light colouresd thread (simply up and down stitches). Sometimes the drawing disappears fast again.

Making and using an iron on pattern

With an iron-on transfert pencil one can copy a pattern on grease-proof paper or tracing paper. One puts the painted side on linen and presses the hot iron on the backside of the paper. Now comes the colour from the paper on the linen. After washing the predrawing is away.

Not enough heat does not iron on,
too much and too long heating up can brown the material.

21

Coral stitch

Mark the motives and embroider the contours with coral stitches. Use a thicker yarn par example size 16 or 20.

Coral stitch:
Take 2 fabric threads on the needle, put the thread from the front around the needle point. Pull the thread a little bit to back.
I work with 2 hands.

This stitch can be embroidered ongoingly and looks like a nodule row.

Chain stitch

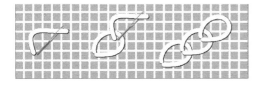

Behind the coral stitch row a row chain stitches is embroidered.

One can embroider the chain stitches also with thick thread (size 16) or a step more fine (size 20).

Finishing a round

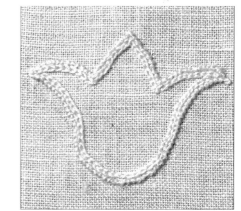

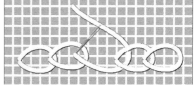

Out drawing of fabric threads

 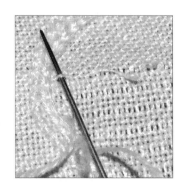 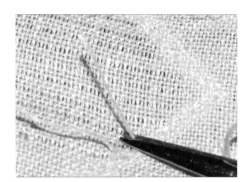

Raising with the needle, cutting through with the scissors and drawing out the thread to both sides.
Cutting the two thread ends off behind - this looks better in front.

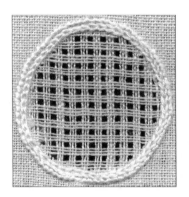

Preparation for the basic stitch:

3 threads remain, draw out 2 threads.

This gives relatively few holes but when embroidering the embroidery goes not out of shape.

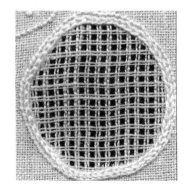

2 threads remain and cut 2 threads.

This gives more holes and you can embroider bigger patterns. But the threads go out of shape, how you can see in the picture.

The basic stitch of schwalm embroidery

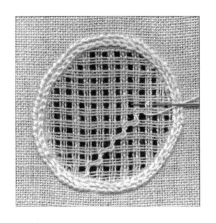 

Embroider diagonally - stitch alternately horizontally and vertically.

Stitch with fine yarn 25 or 30 and with no pointed needle.

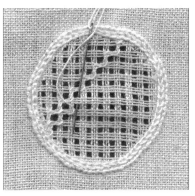 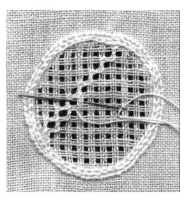

Turn the embroidery and stitch again diagonally alternately horizontally and vertically.

WEAVING PATTERN FILLINGS
also called « Lichte Muster «

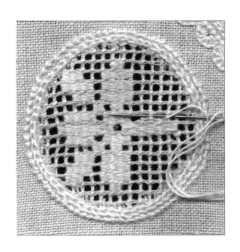

For darning use special
embroidery thread size 20,
more thick.

There are 2 variations:
You can weave horizontally over the thick bars back and forth.

Or you can stretch first a thread horizontally from the left to the
right and then you weave from the right to the left vertically over
the thick bars and the stretched thread.

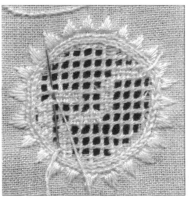

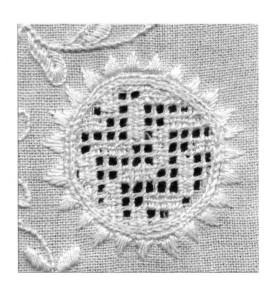

Patterns for 11 holes

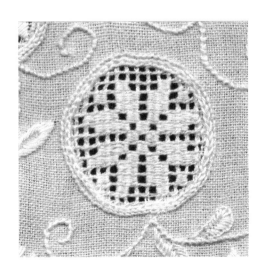

Patterns for 13 holes

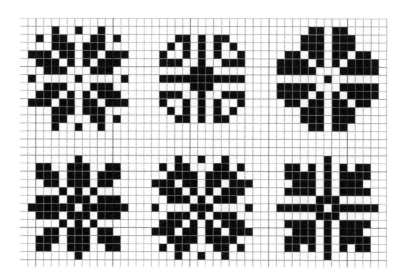

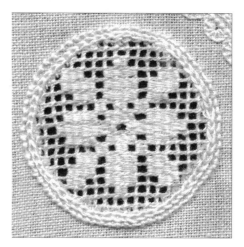

Patterns for 15 holes

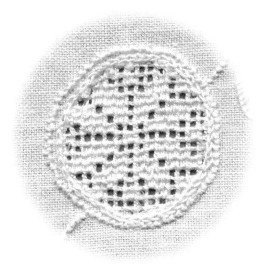
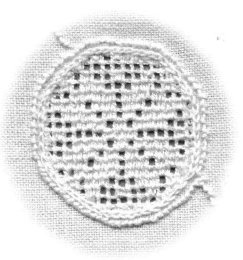

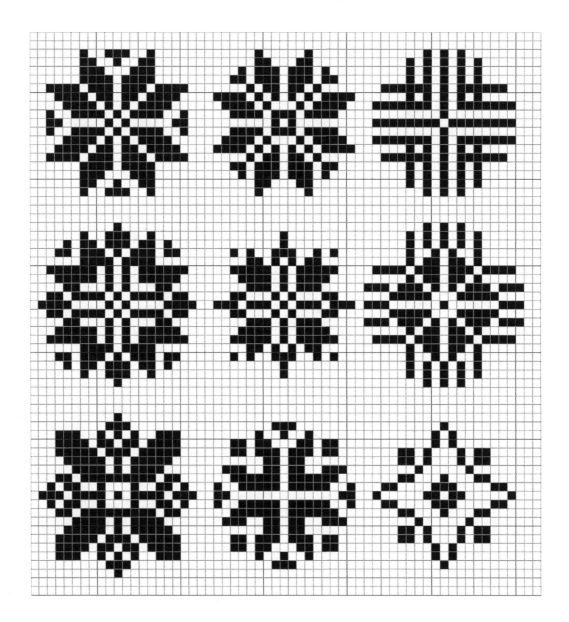

For circles with approx. 8 cm of diameter
by 40 ct linen.

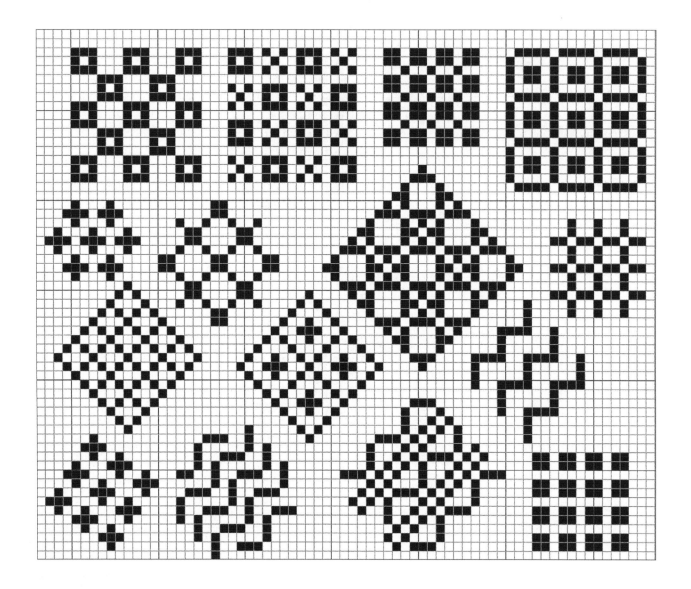

How these endless patterns embroidered look like

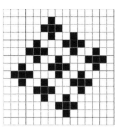

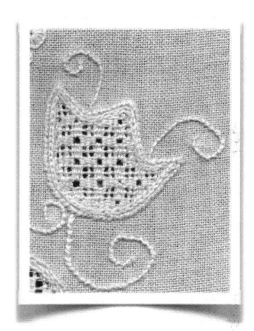

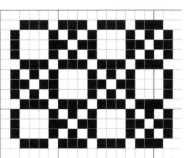

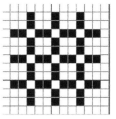

Big « Lichte Muster «

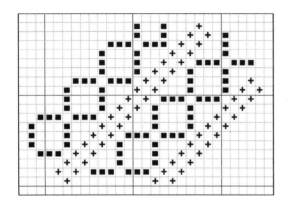

■ to darn,   + rose stitch

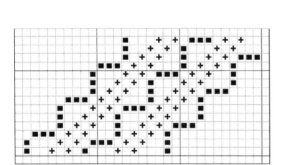

Basic stitch: Rose stitch, « Roeschenstich »

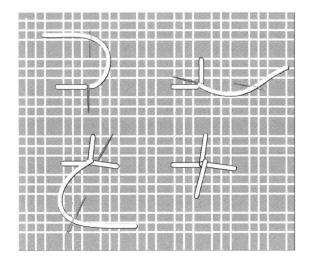

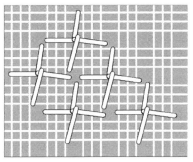

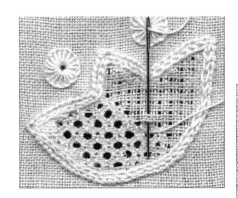

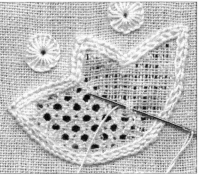

Embroidered with fine cotton 25 or 30 and not pointed needle.

35

« Roeserich «

A relative difficult and complicated pattern, you make diagonally rose stitches and the spaces are in front surrounded with back stitches and then on the back pulled together to get small dimensional elevations.

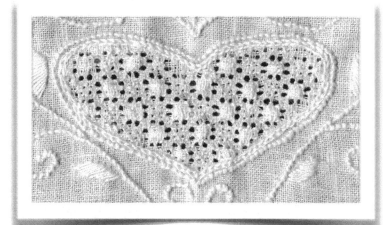

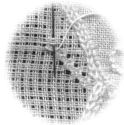

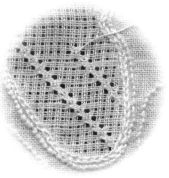

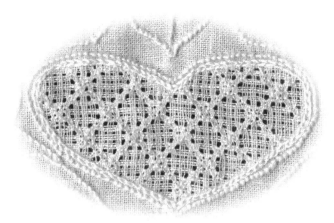

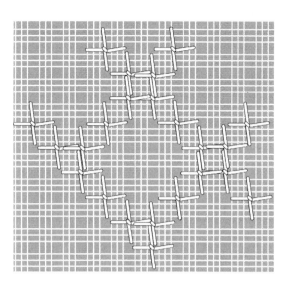

Work rose stitches diagonally in
both directions, parts overlap.

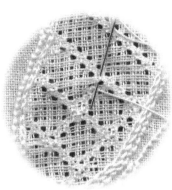

Turn the embroidery and pull on
the backside the backstitches
diagonally together. End with a
knot.
. This upholsters and gives
the three-dimensional effect.

Back stitches around the free fabric
threads.

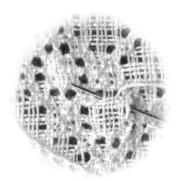

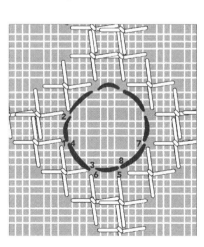

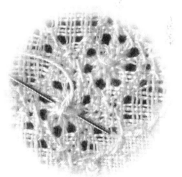

Variation of rose stitch

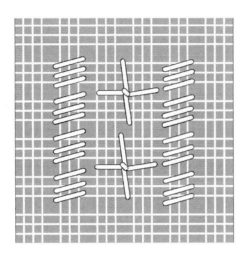

Next variation of rose stitch

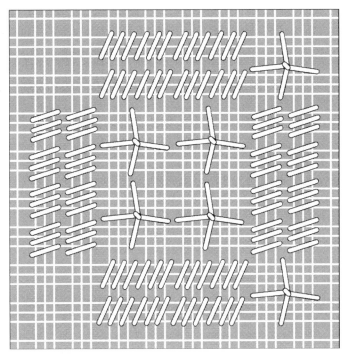

Embroidered with special embroidery
thread size 25

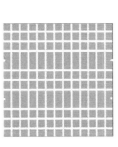

The mosquito stitch

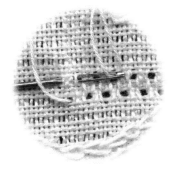

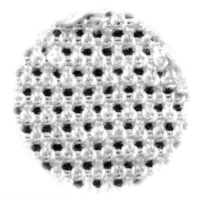

The mosquito stitch is a zig-zag stitch:

VVVVV

Start at the point of a V and work rows from right to left.
At the end of the row turn the work and embroider a new
row.

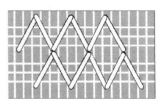

Marburg basic stitch

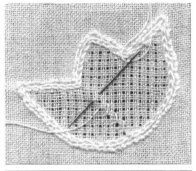
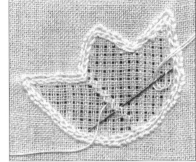

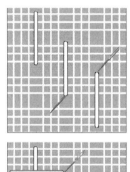

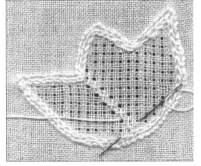
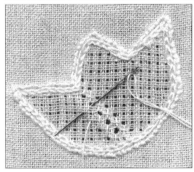

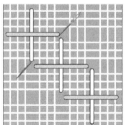

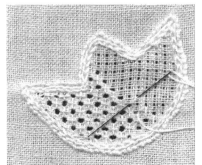

Stitched with thin thread 25
on 35ct linen.

This pattern is easy and
quickly embroidered

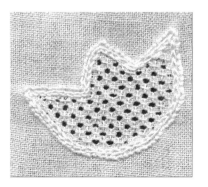

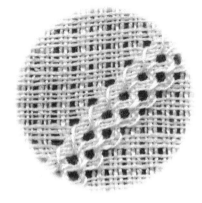

Pattern Lydia

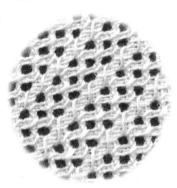

1 row Marburg basic stitch,
2 rows Schwalm basic stitch,
than again 1 row marburg basic stitch and
2 rows Schalm basic stitch.

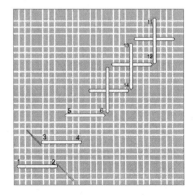

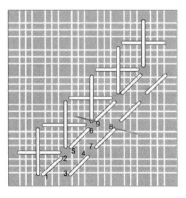

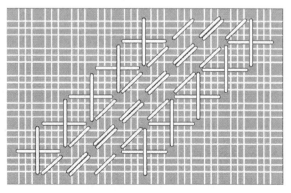

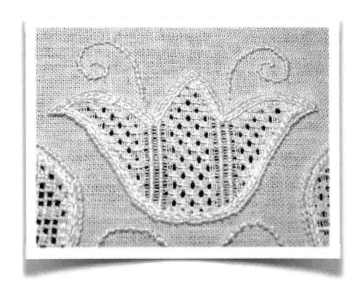
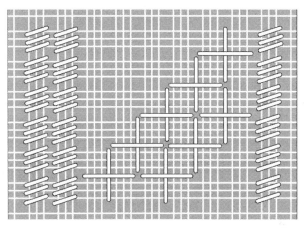

2 Variations with Marburg basic stitch

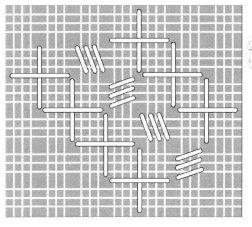

Wafer stitch

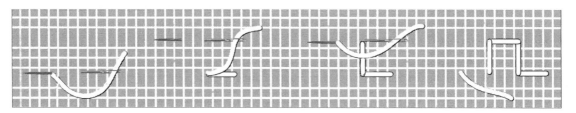

Take 3 fabric threads on the needle, pull the embroidery thread though the linen and stitch again around the same 3 fabric threads. Also stitch alternately above and below twice around 3 fabric threads.

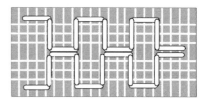

« LIMETROSEN « PATTERNS

patterns with satin stitches

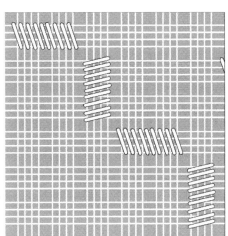

step pattern

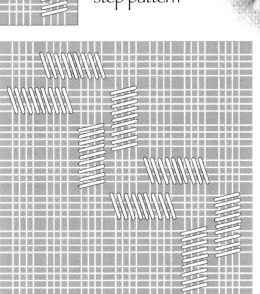

Embroidered with size 25

45

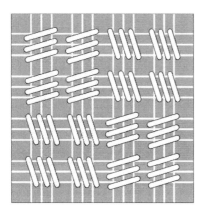

Pattern
with 2 rows

Pattern with 3 rows

46

Rosettes and diamonds

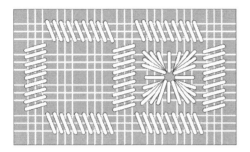

Stitch steps and fill with rosettes.

Rosette pattern
called « Limetrose »

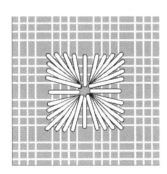

Satin stitch patterns in general are called
« Limetrosen » patterns, but, actually, this rosette is
the « Limetrose ».

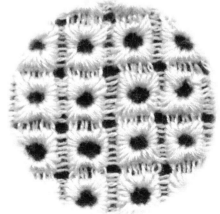

Variation rosette pattern
with oblique thread run,
with obliquely put heart

This pattern is very time consuming .
Embroidered with special embroidery thread 25 on
40ct linen.

Shifted rosettes

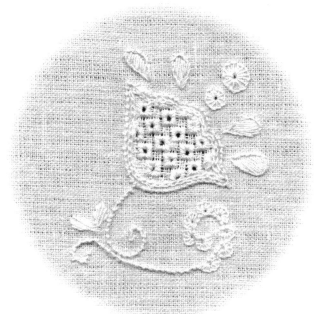

48

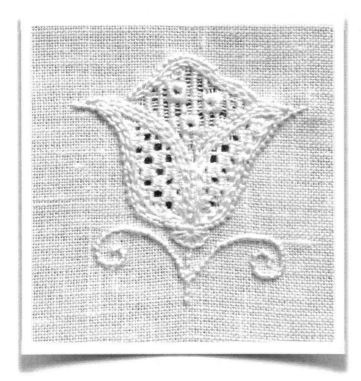

Variation with rosettes and satin stitch rows

The pattern at the top in the tulip:

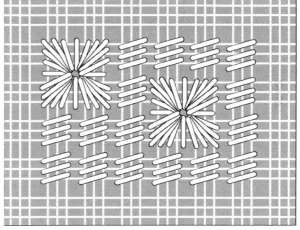

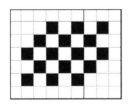

The stitch below in the tulip is a darning pattern described on page 26.

2 threads are drawn out,
2 remain.

If one embroiders like here 2 patterns closely side by side, it can be that with the thread pulling also threads slip out in the other field. Has also happened to me here, but fortunately not to see.

Chessboard pattern

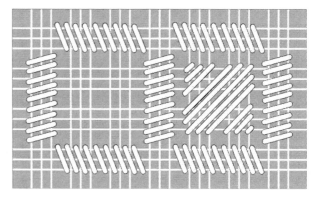

Combination of satin stitch diamonds and satin stitch rows

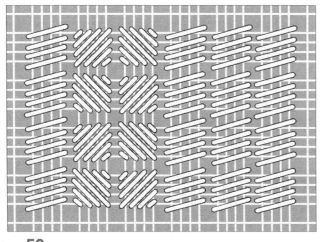

50

Very big chessboard pattern

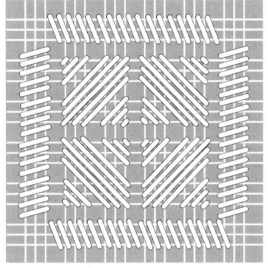

This heart ist big
3.5 x 4 inch
Otherwise so much
pattern does not fit in
the heart

Big chessboard pattern

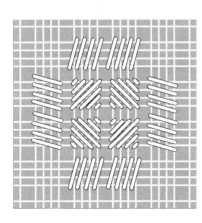

Here I draw every 5. thread

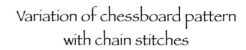

Variation of chessboard pattern
with chain stitches

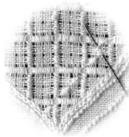

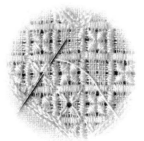

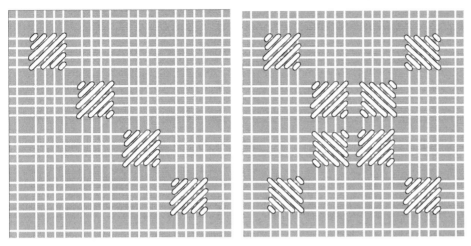

Waffle iron pattern

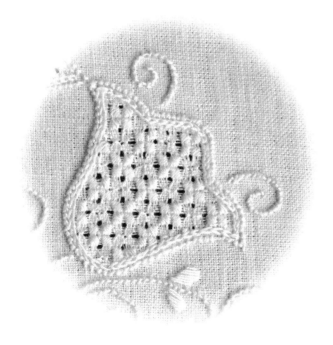

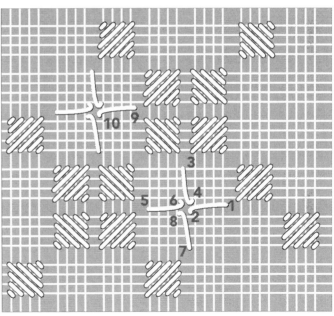

53

Satin stitch rows and rose stitches

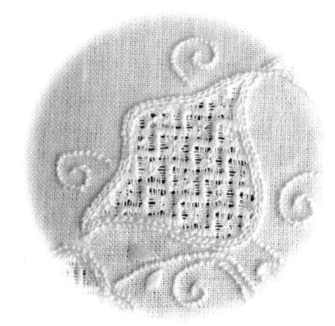

A pattern for bigger surfaces

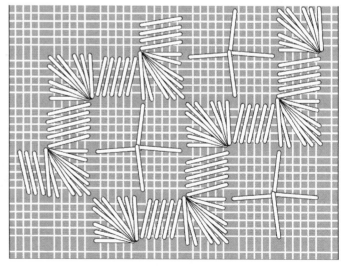

Variation cellar window

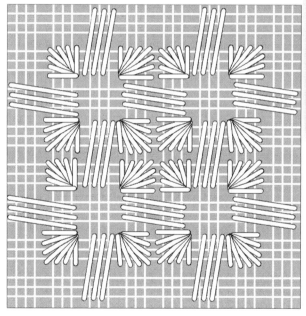

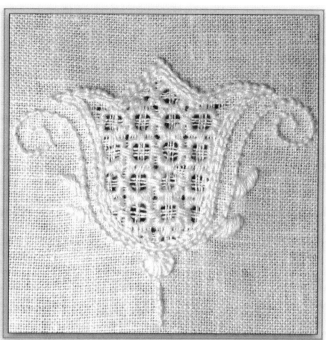

Plumage

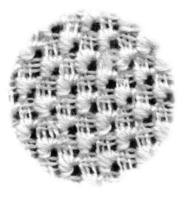

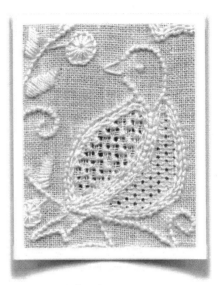

left: plumage,
right: mosquito stitch

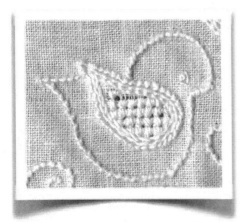

Here I stitched the pattern close
together.

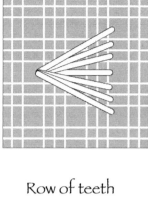

Row of teeth

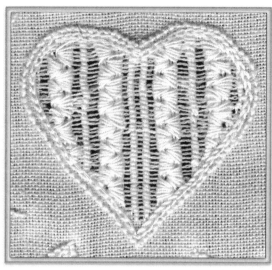

Row of teeth and satin stitch rows

above embroidered with size 20
down with size 25

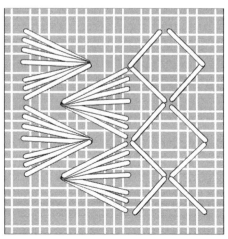

Row of teeth
and mosquito
stitch

Decorations - borders

The motives can be decorated just as you like, with coral stitches,
chain stitches, straight stitches or buttonhole stiches.

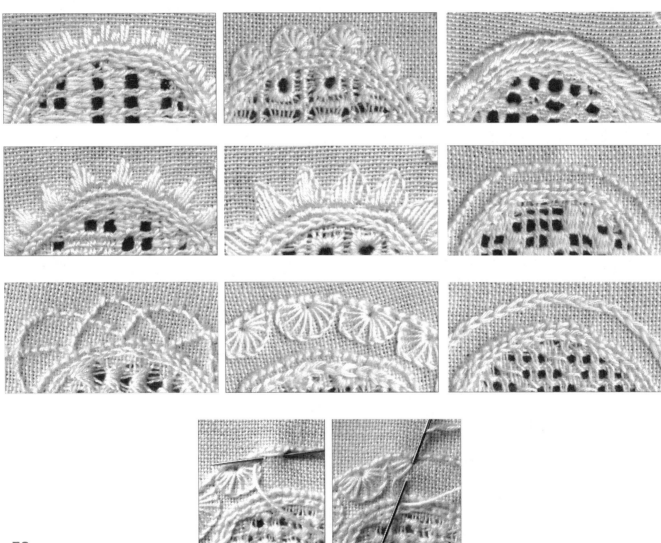

Borders

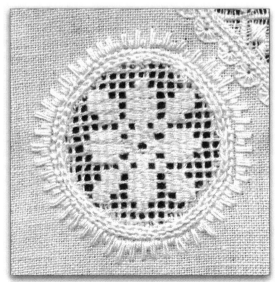

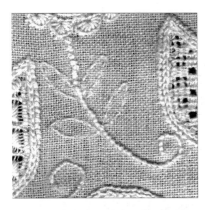

Embroidering leaves

Embroider the form of the leave for preparation with little up-and-down stitches. This gives more hold to the border, but is not urgently necessary.

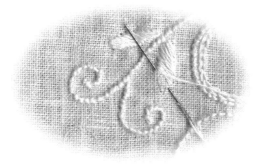

The leaves can be filled with satin stitches.

If you like you can add a border of steem stitches.

This variant to embroider is a little more simply than filling out as in the monogram embroidery. The satin stitches are embroidered from the edge only a piece far in the leave, an open trace remains in the middle.

Leaves of buttonhole stitches are very easy.

Embroider on top in the curve several stitches in one hole.

DECORATIONS

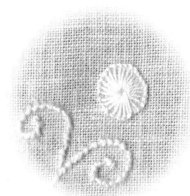

« Das Schnürloch »
buttonhole wheel,

 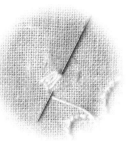 

Tendrils and arcs of coral stitches

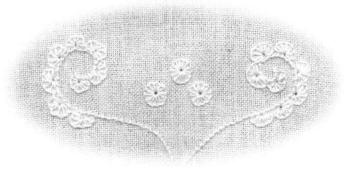

Little flowers

61

Small perfume sachet

approx. 2.7 x 3.9 inches
Embroidered on linen Newcastle of Zweigart and
special embroidery thread 20, 25 und 30

20 for coral stitches,
25 for darning and
30 for Schwalm basic stitch and hem.

Small perfume sachet

2x pieces of linen
3.1 x 5.9 inch

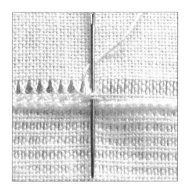

Hemstitch:
Put 3 threads on the needle and come up 2 fabric threads down.

Hemstitch row:

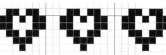

4 threads draw out,
make up and down a row of hemstitches,
make a row of coral stitches,

draw 8 x 2 threads, between let remain 2 threads. Draw 2 threads, 2 remain first vertically and than horizontally.

Row of coral stitches,
hem stitch row.
4 threads out,
hemstitch row.

The cushion of the front and from behind.
Instruction of closure - see page 100

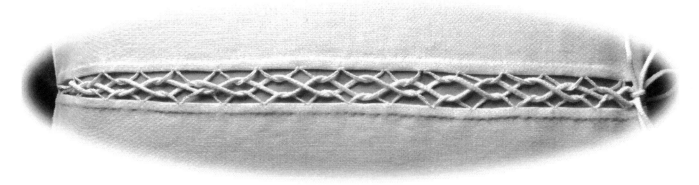

In this size I use it for the model on linen with stripes.

The smaller variation

Pillow approx. 22.4 x 10,2 inch with needleweaving hem, sewn-in laundry lace and tucks

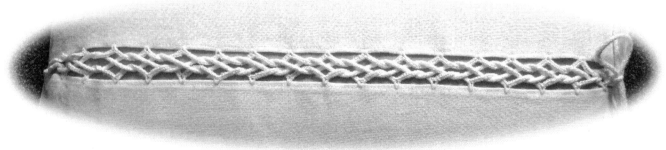

In this size I use the motive for my pillow.

Square pillow

inner part 15.7 x 15,7 inch

Ring pillows with Schwalm embroidery

inside approx. 8 x 8 inch, outside approx. 10 x 10 cm,
made on Zweigart Newcastle with 40ct.

Ring cushion

A n other motive for a ring cushion

One can leave out gladly squiggles and curls or add leaves and other decorations.

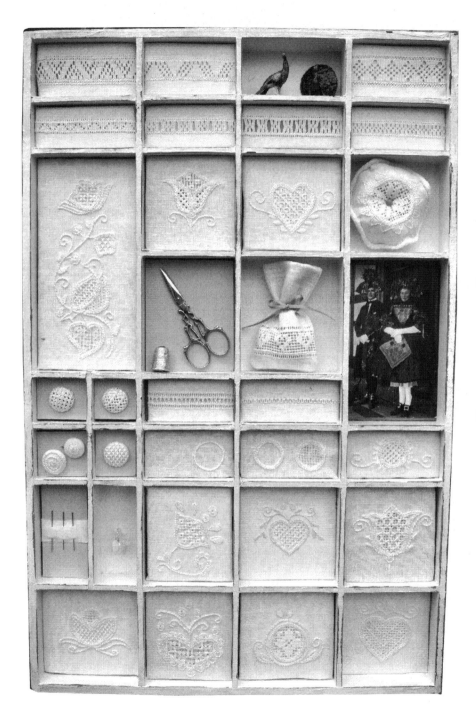

A lettre case with little embroidery motives

The cases are about 3.1 x 3.5 or 1.5 x 3.5 inch.

For the embroideries I cut 2 or 3 small cardboard pieces which are approx. 2mm smaller in all directions as the cases. 1 or 2 as a base, around the upper I cover the embroidery.

I put on one of the pieces a piece of coloured cardboard and on it the embroidery. Now I pull at the back first two sides with long thread and zigzag stitches together. I turn and bring the embroidery in position. Now I pull the other both sides together.

The base card boards and the embroidery are connected with double-sided adhesive tape.

For a lettre case or little doily, greeting card, sachet

I offer the motives in 2 dimensions, you get other
dimensions by bigger copying

AND NOW A FEW MORE PROJECTS

You can scan them and increase or copy more largely.
Or take these arrangements as basic ideas and decorate them just as you like.

Here only the tulips and perhaps the small field above the heart
are to fill with stitch patterns.

A corner motive which can also be used for a doily.

92

The kringles are for buttonhole wheels.
The sun at the top can be decorated outside with curves or points.

2 variations of borders

This motive can be worked continuously.

Tulip border

Of a pillow pattern one can make a table cloth motive by extending.

A few possibilities of extensions

PILLOW CLOSURES FOR COUNTRY HOUSE PILLOWS

Laced pillow closure

Tight for the arcs special embroidery thread size 16
4 times and stitch over this buttonhole stitches. The arcs have a size
of about 1.1 inch.

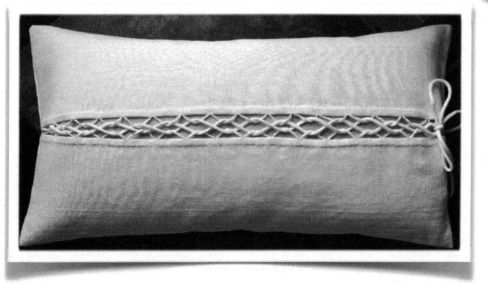

I bind with a cotton cord. For a
pillow of 20 inch width I take 60
inch of cord.

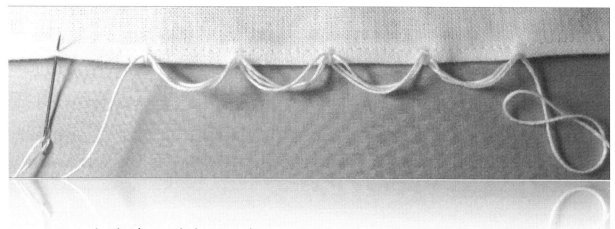

One can do the bound closure also so:

Draw along the open edge all 1.1inch markings.

Take a long thread and start in the midth.
I use a crochet yarn size 10.

Span for each basis arc the thread 3 times and
then make a small firm stitch for securing.

Now crochet with the crochet yarn and single
chains from the front to the back over all arcs.

Length of the cord: 3x the width of
the cushion

Sewed cushion

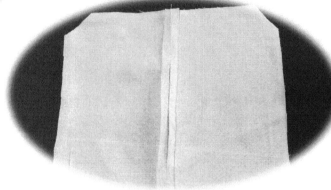

Cut for the back 2 parts and sew them with big
stitches together. Iron the seem addition separated.
Put the back right on the right on the front and sew
everything together. Cut the edges.
Open the middle seem, turn the pillow, stitch a wide
edge strip and fill the pilow with a batting.
Close the seem backside by hand.

Closure with botton and loop

EMBROIDERED BUTTONS

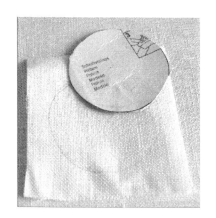

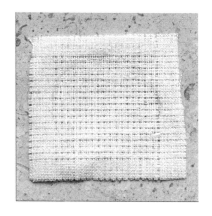

The buttons for covering are from Prym. In the packing is an exact manual in several languages.

Here I work with buttons of 23mm diameter and the small down has 19mm.

Made in the USA
Las Vegas, NV
02 June 2022

49653725R00059